Best Easy Day Hikes Series

Best Easy Day Hikes
Hawaii: Oahu

Suzanne Swedo

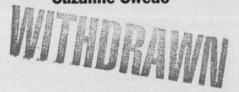

FALCONGUIDES

GUILFORD, CONNECTICUT
HELENA, MONTANA

AN IMPRINT OF GLOBE PEQUOT PRESS

FALCONGUIDES®

Copyright © 2010 by Morris Book Publishing, LLC

FalconGuides is an imprint of Globe Pequot Press.
Falcon, FalconGuides, and Outfit Your Mind are registered trademarks
of Morris Book Publishing, LLC.

Project editor: Julie Marsh
Layout artist: Kevin Mak
Maps: Design Maps Inc. © Morris Book Publishing, LLC
TOPO! Explorer software and SuperQuad source maps courtesy of
National Geographic Maps. For information about TOPO! Explorer,
TOPO!, and Nat Geo Maps products, go to www.topo.com or www
.natgeomaps.com.

Library of Congress Cataloging-in-Publication Data
Swedo, Suzanne, 1945-
  Best easy day hikes, Hawaii, Oahu / Suzanne Swedo.
    p. cm.
  ISBN 978-0-7627-4351-3
  1. Hiking—Hawaii—Oahu—Guidebooks. 2. Trails—Hawaii—Oahu—
Guidebooks. 3. Oahu (Hawaii)—Guidebooks. I. Title.
  GV199.42.H320148 2010
  919.69'3—dc22

                                        2010011380

Printed in the United States of America

10 9 8 7 6 5 4 3 2 1

For Jan Murphy

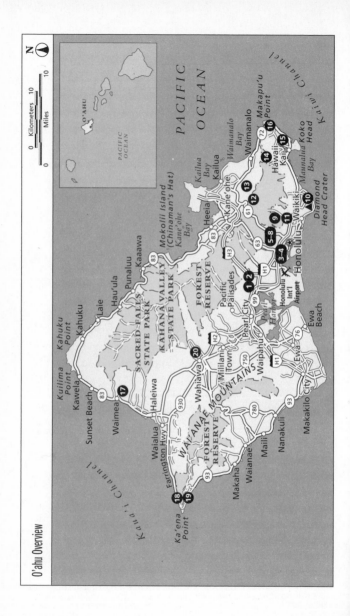

O'ahu Overview

Contents

Introduction

O'ahu, home of Honolulu and Waikiki Beach, is the place that most often comes to mind when you think of Hawai'i. Honolulu became the state capital, as well as the population, business, and visitor center of all the islands, in the days when travel and trade were by sea because of its beautiful harbor. It's a busy city with awful rush hour traffic, jammed with tourist hotels, glitzy shops, and crowded beaches. Much of the land on the rest of the island not devoted to commerce or tourism is military property. Still, O'ahu has a surprising number of very fine hiking trails, most of which are maintained by the *Na Ala Hele* Trail and Access System, part of the state's Division of Forestry and Wildlife. The Web site www.hawaiitrails.org is a great source of information about hiking on the island.

Geologically, O'ahu is the third largest and, not coincidentally, the third youngest of the main Hawaiian islands, formed by two volcanoes, the first of which erupted three to four million years ago. All that is left of this volcano is the Wai'anae Range, the smaller of the two, though its summit, Mount Ka'ala, is O'ahu's highest point at 4,025 feet. The younger volcano, whose remains make up the Ko'olau Range, erupted a million years later, but experienced a more recent spurt of activity 30,000 years ago when it built the cones of Diamond Head, Koko Head, and the Punchbowl. Sediment eroded from the two volcanoes has washed down into the center of the island to form a plateau between them.

As on all the Hawaiian islands, the mountains and the trade winds determine most outdoor activity on O'ahu.

The long Ko'olau Range, which runs from northeast to southwest, blocks the trades, whose moisture carves deep green canyons on the windward side and keeps the central plateau and the leeward coast relatively dry. Hiking the canyons and ridgetops of the windward coast is often wet, but the views through the clouds down to the shoreline are spectacular and the forests display an incredible variety of tropical vegetation. The southeastern peninsula, culminating in Makapu'u Point, is sunny and dry enough to harbor a botanical garden devoted to desert species. The best and most extensive trail system is not far from Honolulu in the foothills of the Ko'olau mountains, where you can put together a hike of any length and difficulty. It can get busy on weekends, but is never really crowded. The most remote and relatively unspoiled hiking can be found at the western end of O'ahu. Ka'ena Point in particular is one of the few places where you can still see the real Hawai'i, including native wildlife.

Maps

The *Na Ala Hele* Trail and Access System publishes free maps of all the trails it administers. These are photocopies of the USGS topographic maps with updated trails added. They are too small for serious navigation, but are helpful as supplements to outdated USGS topos. Call (808) 973-9782 for copies, or better, visit www.hawaiitrails.org.

The shaded relief map of O'ahu published by the University of Hawai'i Press, available in bookstores and elsewhere, is the best for exploring the island as a whole. It gives you a bird's-eye view of the geography of the island, including its mountains, waterfalls, beaches, and of course, its roads and highways. It does not, however, have the detail you need to navigate your way around the bewildering maze of Honolulu, so a good street map, such as the one published by AAA, is also essential.

Getting Around

O'ahu offers public transportation in the form of TheBus, which is very useful for getting around Honolulu and Waikiki. But TheBus does not go to most trailheads so if you don't live here, you'll need to rent a car. It's too bad, because Honolulu has one of the most illogical, confusing, maddening road and freeway systems ever! You can get a schedule for TheBus at www.thebus.org or by calling (808) 848-5555, or pick one up at any number of locations in the city.

Accommodations

There are a surprising number of inexpensive hotels and hostels all over O'ahu, even in Waikiki. There are many campgrounds, too, all of which require a permit. Information about camping and permits at in Honolulu's city and county parks is available at (808) 768-3440 or www.co .honolulu.hi.us/parks. For camping at state parks call (808) 587-0300. Online reservations are not accepted.

A Few Words of Caution

Lava

Lava weathers to red clay over time—easy enough walking when dry, but after a hard rain it becomes as slippery as butter on glass. Hikes may become much more difficult when the weather is bad. Narrow footpaths clinging to mountain-sides can become downright dangerous. Hiking sticks and good shoes are recommended.

Weather Patterns

Weather in Hawai'i is usually lovely, with temperatures between 70 and 80 degrees year-round. There are essentially two seasons. Summer (May through October) is only slightly warmer than winter. The trade winds blowing from the northeast usually keep even the warmer days pleasant. Rainfall is lighter and of shorter duration in summer than in winter. Rainfall in winter is more frequent, heavier, and lasts longer, but is not likely to spoil most hikes unless there is a Kona storm. These occur when for some reason the trade winds fail. Kona storms come from the opposite direction than the trade winds, the southwest instead of the northeast, and it can rain buckets for days on end.

Pack plenty of layers, some of them synthetic rather than cotton for fast drying and wicking moisture away from your skin. A Windbreaker and rain gear are essential items to carry in your day pack. Make sure you have a brimmed hat and lots of sunscreen, too. The sun is directly overhead this close to the equator.

Drinking Water

All free-flowing water on the islands must be treated before drinking. In Hawai'i, leptospirosis is the most significant waterborne disease-causing organism. It is spread primarily by rats, mice, and mongooses. It is a bacterium that can cause flu-like symptoms including fever, diarrhea, nausea, muscle pain, chills, headache, and weakness, and if not treated with antibiotics can lead to very serious problems like heart or kidney failure.

Chemical treatment or boiling will take care of drinking water, but you can get leptospirosis by swimming in contaminated water as well as by drinking it. You are advised not to swim in fresh water if you have a cut or broken skin, and not to put your head underwater. That said, swimming and splashing in Hawaii's streams and pools is one of the most popular pastimes in the islands, and nobody appears to be overly concerned. But you should be aware that there is a risk.

Stream Crossings

Speaking of water, it rains a lot on windward O'ahu and there are several hikes in this guide that involve stream crossings. Some are shallow enough to rock hop, though rocks are usually rounded and slick, and wading is safer. If it has been raining long and hard streams may be too high and fast to ford safely. Unexpected flash floods are especially dangerous and have killed lots of people. Many of Hawaii's streams flow down almost perpendicular cliffs, and floods may originate high up in the rainy mountains while you stroll unaware along the coast under sunny skies. If a stream appears muddy, or if you can hear rocks rolling along the streambed, turn around! Tropical vegetation often releases tannins into water, making it dark in color and hard to see through even under ordinary conditions, but swirling mud is serious.

Waves, Currents, and Riptides

The seas around the islands have weird patterns. There are lovely quiet coves perfect for snorkeling and big regular waves for surfing, but in some places riptides can pull you off your feet and sweep you out to sea in an instant. Never turn your back to the ocean when exploring tide pools or walking along sea cliffs. A rogue wave can sneak up on you any time.

Beaches where it is not safe to swim are almost always clearly marked with warning signs, and they mean business!

Hawai'i has experienced tsunamis (tidal waves) at rare intervals in its history that killed many. You will probably notice yellow civil defense warning sirens on posts all over windward coastlines. If these begin to blow, get to higher ground immediately.

Losing the Trail

Established trails are usually easy to follow. If there is any ambiguity the clearest, most defined trail is usually the right one. Sometimes trails are so badly eroded by hikers, each going a separate way to avoid mud puddles or deep holes, that new mud puddles and deep holes are created. Eventually a network of false paths obscures the correct route. Stay alert and look beyond worn spots to find where the trail picks up again. If you are uncertain about which path to take, try one for a short distance. If it seems to lead nowhere turn around and go back to where you began, then start over. Don't compound a mistake by plunging farther and farther into the unknown.

In Hawai'i it is especially important to stay on trails—maybe more so than in other places—because thick undergrowth can mask deep cracks or overhangs and dense forest vegetation can obscure boundaries of private property. Many routes skirt or cross private property whose owners have granted hikers the right of way, but a *kapu* (prohibition or taboo) sign means no trespassing.

Pig and goat hunting are time-honored pastimes in the islands. At present, hunting is permitted in certain areas on O'ahu on weekends and holidays, but schedules change. Areas where hunting is allowed will usually have a sign saying so at the trailhead. If you stay on the trail and wear bright clothing there is very little danger from hunters.

Sticking to the trail will also help you respect cultural traditions by steering you away from religious sites and cemeteries.

Trailhead Vandalism

Vandalism is the most distressing, even if not life-threatening, experience most hikers ever face. For the most part, Hawaiians are friendly, helpful, and kind. Unfortunately, there is poverty and resentment here as everywhere, and tourists are easy marks. Rental cars are usually obvious, and tourists are apt to leave all sorts of belongings in them when they go off for a hike.

If you are about to pull into a parking space at a remote trailhead and see broken glass on the ground, be warned. Leave absolutely nothing in your car, even in the trunk. You might consider leaving the doors unlocked to avoid having a window broken, although even that doesn't always work. Isolated trailheads where no one will hear breaking glass are the worst. Busy trailheads with people coming and going all day are safer, as are trailheads in national parks. Overnight parking at trailheads is risky anywhere, but especially near a big population center.

But don't spoil your visit by worrying about your car. The odds against any problems are in your favor, and you can greatly improve them by taking a few precautions.

Zero Impact

We, as trail users, must be vigilant to make sure our passage leaves no lasting mark. Here are some basic guidelines for preserving trails in the region:

- Pack out all your own trash. You might also pack out garbage left by less-considerate hikers.

- Don't approach or feed any wild creatures—the crow eyeing your snack food is best able to survive if it remains self-reliant.

- Don't pick wildflowers or gather rocks, feathers, or other treasures along the trail. Removing these items will only take away from the next hiker's experience.

- Avoid damaging trailside soils and plants by remaining on the established route.

- Be courteous by not making loud noises while hiking.

- Many of these trails are multiuse, which means you'll share them with other hikers, trail runners, mountain bikers, and equestrians. Familiarize yourself with the proper trail etiquette, yielding the trail when appropriate.

- Use outhouses at trailheads or along the trail.

How to Use This Guide

To aid in quick decision making, each hike chapter begins with a hike summary. These short summaries give you a taste of the hiking adventure to follow and what surprises the route has to offer. Next, you'll find the quick, nitty-gritty details of the hike: where the trailhead is located, hike length, approximate hiking time, type of trail terrain, what other trail users you may encounter, trail contacts (for updates on trail conditions), and trail schedules and usage fees. No need for difficulty ratings since all hikes are "easy"—under 5 miles in length, minimal elevation gain, and relatively even terrain (except in the rainy season when most will be muddy).

The approximate hiking times are based on a standard hiking pace of 1.5 to 2 miles per hour, adjusted for terrain and reflecting normal trail conditions. The stated times will get you there and back, but be sure to add time for rest breaks and enjoying the trail's attractions. Although the stated times offer a planning guideline, you should gain a sense of your personal health, capabilities, and hiking style and make this judgment for yourself. If you're hiking with a group, add enough time for slower members. The amount of carried gear also will influence hiking speed. In all cases leave enough daylight to accomplish the task safely.

The **Finding the trailhead** section gives you dependable directions from a nearby city or town right down to where you'll want to park your car. The hike description is the meat of the chapter. Detailed and honest, it's the author's carefully researched impression of the trail. While it's impossible to cover everything, you can rest assured that we won't miss what's important. In **Miles and Directions** we provide mileage cues to key junctions and trail name changes, as well as points of interest. The selected benchmarks allow for a quick check on progress and serve as your touchstone for staying on course.

Most maps in this book indicate the general route of the hike. However, in some cases, the route is not well-defined so the map shows you how to reach the trailhead.

How to Speak Hawaiian

The Hawaiian language has only twelve letters: the vowels a, e, i, o, and u, and the consonants h, k, l, m, n, p, and w. It also has a diacritical mark, the glottal stop (indicated by an apostrophe), that tells you how to separate the syllables. The apostrophe gives spoken Hawaiian its distinctive sound and rhythm. For example, chunky lava, *a'a,* is not pronounced "aaah," but "ah-ah." The word Hawai'i itself has a glottal stop, and you probably already know how to say it: "Howai-ee." If two vowels are not separated by a glottal stop, they are pronounced together, like the "ai" in Hawai'i.

Here are a few words you will hear over and over on Hawai'i. Many refer to physical features of the land and help interpret the names of significant landmarks:

pu'u = hill

mauna = mountain

a'a = rough, chunky lava

pahoehoe = smooth, ropy lava

mauka = toward the mountain

makai = toward the sea

loa = long

kea = white

pali = cliff

heiau = holy place

lua = hole or toilet

kokua = please or help

mahalo = thank you

kapu = taboo, forbidden, keep out

aloha = hello, good-by, love

Hike Ratings

All hikes in this guide are easy, but some are more strenuous than others. The list below rates hikes from easiest to most challenging.

Easiest

>   Lili'uokalani Botanical Garden (Hike 4)
>   Pu'u o Mahuka Heiau (Hike 17)
>   Foster Botanical Garden (Hike 3)
>   Wahiawa Botanical Garden (Hike 20)
>   Lyon Arboretum (Hike 6)
>   Koko Crater Botanical Garden (Hike 15)
>   Nu'uanu Pali–The Old Pali Highway (Hike 12)
>   Tantalus-Arboretum Trail (Hike 7)
>   Judd–Jackass Ginger Pool (Hike 11)
>   Kuli'ou'ou Valley Trail (Hike 14)
>   Waimano Valley (Hike 1)
>   Ka Iwi (Makapu'u Point) (Hike 16)
>   Ka'ena Point North (Hike 18)
>   Ka'ena Point South (Hike 19)
>   Manoa Falls (Hike 5)
>   Maunawili Falls (Hike 13)
>   Pu'u Ohia (Mount Tantalus) (Hike 8)
>   Pu'u Pia (Hike 9)
>   Diamond Head (Hike 10)
>   'Aiea Loop (Hike 2)

More challenging

Map Legend

═══(H1)═══	Interstate Highway
──(83)──	State Highway
───────	Local Road
=======	Unpaved Road
├──────┤	Tunnel
- - - - - -	Trail
▬▬▬▬▬▬	Featured Trail
～～～	River/Creek
🪨	Body of Water
░▲░	Local/State Park
░▲░	Forest Reserve/State Park
✕	Airport
≍	Bridge
⊛	Capital
•─•	Gate
🗼	Lighthouse
🅿	Parking
▲	Peak
■	Point of Interest/Structure
🚻	Restroom
○	Town
11	Trailhead
🔰	Viewpoint/Overlook
❓	Visitor/Information Center
🚰	Water
≋	Waterfall

1 Waimano Valley

There are lots of wild fruits and berries along this trail. The loop is a short sample of the much longer Waimano Trail, which struggles steeply up toward the rainy Ko'olau mountains. Overlooks along the upper section offer vistas over a patchwork of lacy textures and colors created by the treetops in Waimano Valley. Once you have descended to the valley floor, walking alongside a little stream, you can experience the forest more intimately from below the canopy.

Distance: 2-mile loop
Elevation change: 200 feet
Approximate hiking time: 45 minutes–1.5 hours
Trail surface: Maintained trail (worn lava) with a few short, steep sections that are slippery when wet
Other trail users: Hunters, mountain bikers
Canine compatibility: Leashed dogs permitted
Fees and permits: None
Schedule: Daily during daylight hours
Land status: Waimano Gulch State Park Reserve
Map: *USGS Waipahu*
Trail contact: Hawai'i Department of Land and Natural Resources; (808) 973-9782; www.hawaiitrails.org

Finding the trailhead: From Honolulu take HI 1 (the Lunalilo Freeway) west to exit 10 for Pearl City. Turn right (west) onto Moanalua Road. Go just over 1 mile to Waimano Home Road and turn right (north). Follow it for 1 mile to the guardhouse and park in wide spots along the road on either side. There is a guard station at the trailhead. The guard is not, of course, responsible for your car, but it would take a very bold or stupid thief to break in. The security guard will also know if hunters are around. **Trailhead GPS:** N21 24.55' / W157 57.23'

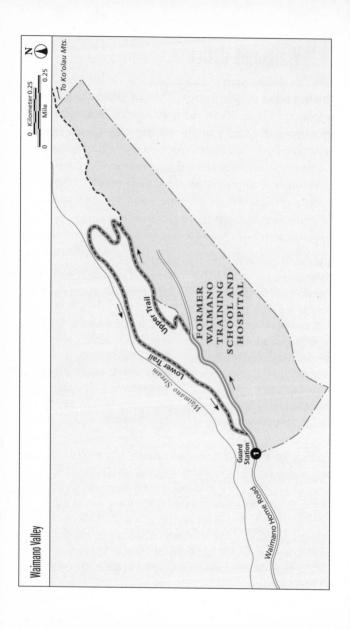

Waimano Valley

N

0 Kilometer 0.25
0 Mile 0.25

To Ko'olau Mts.

FORMER
WAIMANO
TRAINING
SCHOOL AND
HOSPITAL

Upper Trail

Lower Trail

Waimano Stream

Guard
Station

Waimano Home Road

The Hike

You can do this hike in either direction, but it is described counterclockwise, beginning on the upper trail and returning on the lower. There are so many kinds of wild fruits and berries along the route, you won't make much forward progress in spring and summer if you try to sample them all. Surinam cherry, strawberry guava, Java plum, and mountain apple are all edible in season. *Do not* try anything you cannot identify with complete confidence.

Pass the guardhouse and begin walking along the road, keeping to the left of a chain-link fence. In just a few paces, the upper and lower trails split. Keep right (east) on the upper trail, which soon veers slightly away from the road. Scramble up an eroded bare dirt gully to an overlook of Waimano Valley for a gorgeous view over the forest with the mountains as backdrop.

Descend a little, and in about 0.5 mile pass a tunnel that was part of an old irrigation system. The trail to the right (south) continues on up the Waimano Valley, becoming more difficult and less distinct. You should turn left (north) at a junction that drops downhill steeply on switchbacks to the lower section of the trail. The route is easy to follow, marked with plastic strips, but somewhat overgrown. Watch your head for low branches.

Veer left (southwest) and go through a tunnel hacked through a thicket of *hau* (pronounced "how"), a kind of hibiscus. Its long branches spread horizontally, putting down roots whenever they touch the soil so that they form a tangled mass of interlocking limbs. Its name is easy to remember: Just ask "*Hau* could anybody get through this without a chainsaw?"

Just beyond the hau tunnel you meet Waimano Stream, along which you stroll through a forest of dwarf bamboo, ferns, fishtail palms, and *kukui* trees. When the path leaves the stream, head gradually uphill on an old road and back to the first junction and the trailhead.

Miles and Directions

0.0   Start

1.0   Junction with the connector to the lower trail; turn left/down-hill (N21 23.23' / W157 56.23')

2.0   Return to the trailhead

2 'Aiea Loop

Just above Honolulu, but high enough into the Ko'olau mountains to feel wild and remote, this relatively level loop is a great favorite with both locals and visitors. In fact, it can be crowded on weekends. There are some interesting views and a variety of tropical trees and flowers. It can be slippery when wet so hiking poles and caution are recommended if it has been raining. There is a *heiau* (sacred site) to visit near the trailhead as an added bonus.

Distance: 4.7-mile loop
Elevation gain: 900 feet
Approximate hiking time: 2-3 hours
Trail surface: Well-maintained lava with some fallen trees and slippery tree roots
Other trail users: Mountain bikers and, rarely, equestrians
Canine compatibility: Dogs permitted
Fees and permits: None

Schedule: Daily during daylight hours
Land status: Keaiwa Heiau State Recreation Area
Maps: USGS *Kaneohe* and *Waipahu*
Trail contact: Hawai'i Department of Land and Natural Resources, Division of State Parks; (808) 587-0166; www .hawaiistateparks.org/parks

Finding the trailhead: Take HI 1 (the Lunalilo Freeway) west to HI 201. The exit is from the left lane. Almost at once, go left (northwest) again onto HI 78. Follow this to the Stadium/'Aiea exit. Turn right toward 'Aiea. Follow Moanalua Road for 2 blocks to 'Aiea Heights Drive. Turn right (north) and wind up and up through suburbs to the Keaiwa Heiau State Recreation Area. Continue as the road becomes one way, and park at the highest point in the road. There is plenty of parking, restrooms, water, a picnic area, and a small brown and gold trail sign. **Trailhead GPS:** N21 23.47' / W157 54.20'

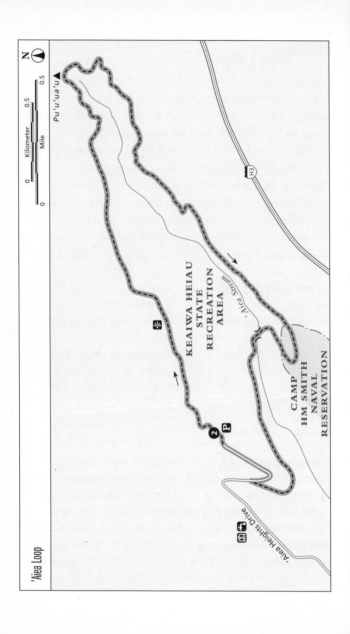

'Aiea Loop

KEAIWA HEIAU
STATE
RECREATION
AREA

CAMP
HM SMITH NAVAL
RESERVATION

'Aiea Heights Drive

'Aiea Stream

H3

Pu'u'ua'u

2

P

N

0   0.5   Kilometer
0   0.5   Mile

The Hike

You can walk the loop in either direction, but most people prefer to start at the upper end and wind up at the lower, so that is how it is described here, in a clockwise direction. Either way, you have to walk back up to your car at the end.

The trail begins at a small brown-and-gold trail sign in a grove of swamp mahogany (a kind of eucalyptus) and travels through a forest of all the usual weedy suspects, like strawberry guava, Cook pine, and ironwood, to an open area of red dirt crisscrossed with tangled tree roots. Take in the view out toward Honolulu from a clearing, then swing left (north) and follow the nearly flat path, ignoring side trails that shoot off here and there. Along with weeds like lantana and the notorious Koster's curse, you'll find orchids and clumps of bamboo. In the steeper, shadier valleys you can still find real Hawaiians like *koa*, and lots of different kinds of ferns.

At about 0.6 mile you can sit on a bench and enjoy a view of a slice of the coast. In another mile you reach the high point of the hike on Pu'u'ua'u at more than 1,600 feet, and just beyond it another bench at which you can sit and enjoy a view of . . . the freeway. The next opening in the trees gives you a look out over a bit of the Salt Pond and Pearl Harbor. There are several fallen trees at intervals on this section of the trail (the farthest from either trailhead) that you must clamber over or scrunch under.

About three-quarters of the way along the loop, you begin to descend through *ti* plants, ginger, and octopus trees with pink arms that stick up like broken umbrellas (or a surprised octopus) when in bloom. Cross the 'Aiea stream-bed and start back uphill again. As you level out, the trail surface changes to what looks like cobblestone paving, actually shells of *kukui* nuts, whose branches are now overhead. Reach another open red dirt spot with a view, swing around a corner, and find yourself at a grassy campground. Climb up the slope beside the restroom to the road, on which you turn right (northeast) and walk back up to your car.

Miles and Directions

0.0 'Aiea Loop Trailhead

1.6 Pu'u'ua'u, the high point on trail (N21 24.20' / W157 52.59')

4.7 Return to 'Aiea Loop Trailhead

3 Foster Botanical Garden

This surprising green oasis is right in the middle of downtown Honolulu. It is the oldest of the five Honolulu Botanical Gardens, each of which protects a different habitat with its own specialized kinds of plants. If you visit them all, you will be surprised at how many widely differing environments exist on this one small island. This one features subtropical and tropical species. It was opened to the public in 1931, but its history goes clear back to 1853. The stupendous size of some of the trees confirms its venerable history.

Distance: Less than 1-mile loop

Elevation change: None

Approximate hiking time: 30 minutes–1 hour

Trail surface: Grass

Other trail users: None

Canine compatibility: Dogs not permitted

Fees and permits: Entry fee

Schedule: Open year-round 9:00 a.m. to 4:00 p.m. daily. Docents lead guided walks at 1:00 p.m. Mon through Sat.

Map: A map is included in the brochure you receive when you enter.

Trail contact: Honolulu Department of Parks and Recreation; (808) 522-7066; www.honolulu.gov/parks/hbg

Finding the trailhead: This is one hike where you can actually use TheBus to get there. Call (808) 848-5555 for route information, or pick up a current schedule at hotels and shops all over Honolulu and Waikiki.

If you are driving from Waikiki, go east on Ala Moana Boulevard (HI 92) to Pau Street, where you make a very short left, then go left (west) again onto Ala Wai Boulevard. In less than 1 mile turn right (north) on McCully Street and cross over HI 1 (the Lunalilo Freeway). Turn left (west) at Dole Street, then left again onto Alexander Street, which merges onto HI 1 westbound. Turn off at Vineyard Boulevard

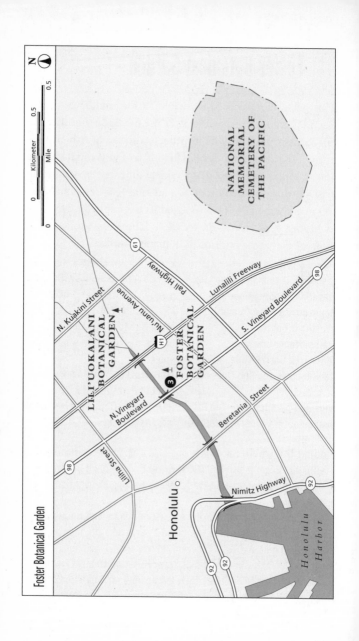

Foster Botanical Garden

N

0   Kilometer   0.5

0   Mile   0.5

NATIONAL
MEMORIAL
CEMETERY OF
THE PACIFIC

61

Pali Highway

Lunalili Freeway

98

N. Kuakini Street

Nuʻuanu Avenue

LILIʻUOKALANI
BOTANICAL
GARDEN

H1

FOSTER
BOTANICAL
GARDEN

3

N. Vineyard Boulevard

S. Vineyard Boulevard

98

Liliha Street

Beretania Street

Honolulu

Nimitz Highway

92

92

92

Honolulu
Harbor

(exit 22) and keep right (north) on South Vineyard to 180 North Vineyard. There is a public parking lot, a small gift shop, and a few exhibits at the entrance. **Trailhead GPS:** N21 18.56' / W157 51.30'

The Hike

The brochure you receive when you go into the garden lists numbered specimens in a lopsided loop going clockwise, but you can wander in any direction you like. Be sure to really look at the brochure and map to the self-guided nature trail, or you might miss some fascinating sights. If you think that having seen one palm tree you've seen them all, just wait!

Before you rush to the entrance, check out the trees in the parking lot. There are some real beauties with extravagantly showy flowers. Upon entering the garden start walking straight ahead toward the Bo (also known as Bodhi) Tree, the tree under which the Buddha is said to have received Enlightenment. As you make a clockwise circuit, you will encounter, among many others, a kapok tree whose size is simply indescribable. You have to stand beside it to believe it, even if you've already seen California redwoods and sequoias.

There are dozens of kinds of palms, including the double coconut, whose seeds, the largest in the world, weigh up to fifty pounds. There is an earpod tree, whose fruits look like the ears of giants; a sausage tree, whose fruits look like enormous sausages dangling from branches on strings; and a cannonball tree with fruits as big as cannonballs growing right out of the trunk instead of hanging from the branches.

Pass through a shady section called the Prehistoric Glen, filled with plants that originated in the time of the dinosaurs, then a patch of economically important trees like macadamia nuts and breadfruits. There are also some beautiful orchids, as well as ornamentals, scattered throughout the grounds.

4 Lili'uokalani Botanical Garden

This is a compact little jewel crammed in among apartment buildings, just right for a stroll and a picnic in the heat of the day.

Distance: 0.3-mile loop
Elevation change: None
Approximate hiking time: 10–30 minutes
Trail surface: Paved sidewalk and grass
Other trail users: None
Canine compatibility: Dogs not permitted

Fees and permits: None
Schedule: Open daily from 7:00 a.m. to 5:00 p.m.
Maps: None needed
Trail contact: Honolulu Department of Parks and Recreation; (808) 522-7060; www.honolulu.gov/parks/hbg

Finding the trailhead: From Waikiki, go east on Ala Moana Boulevard (HI 92) to Pau Street, where you make a very short left, then a left (west) again onto Ala Wai Boulevard. In less than 1 mile, turn right (north) on McCully Street and cross over HI 1 (the Lunalilo Freeway). Turn left (west) at Dole Street, then left again onto Alexander Street, which merges into HI 1 westbound. Turn off at Vineyard Boulevard (exit 22) and keep right (north) on South Vineyard to Nu'uanu Avenue, where you turn right (northeast). Cross the freeway and go 4 blocks to North Kuakini Street and turn left (northwest); the park entrance is about 1 block down on your left (southeast). There is no street number. Street parking is available. **Trailhead GPS:** N21 19.09' / W157 21.20'

The Hike

This quiet little garden is within easy walking distance of the Foster Botanical Garden (though you can drive if you

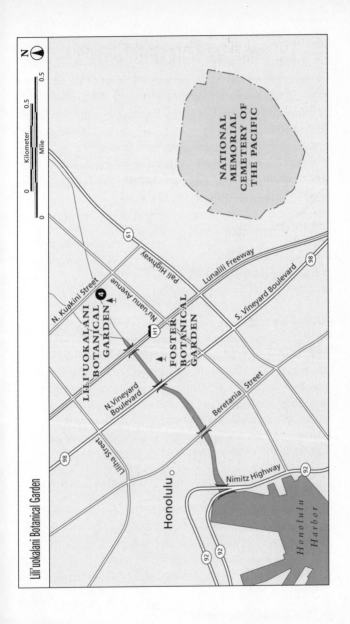

Lili'uokalani Botanical Garden

N

0   Kilometer   0.5

0   Mile   0.5

NATIONAL
MEMORIAL
CEMETERY OF
THE PACIFIC

61

Pali Highway

Lunalili Freeway

98

N. Kuakini Street

Nu'uanu Avenue

LILI'UOKALANI
BOTANICAL
GARDEN

4

H1

S. Vineyard Boulevard

FOSTER
BOTANICAL
GARDEN

N. Vineyard
Boulevard

Beretania Street

98

Liliha Street

Honolulu

Nimitz Highway

92

92

92

Honolulu
Harbor

like). It was a favorite of Queen Lilioukalani, the last reigning monarch of Hawai'i, who bequeathed it to Honolulu for everyone to enjoy. It has a grassy lawn to stroll along, planted with native Hawaiian plants with identifying labels. Its best feature is a stream that tumbles over a little waterfall and splashes through the middle of the park from end to end. At the upper end are some big old banyan trees whose curtains of aerial roots screen the park from the city outside. You can cross the stream on a bridge and picnic on the lawn, as do many of the locals at lunchtime.

5 Manoa Falls

This is one of the prettiest and most popular hikes on O'ahu. It's a perfect family ramble along a stream amid lush tropical vegetation to a waterfall and pool.

Distance: 1.6 miles out and back
Elevation gain: 750 feet
Approximate hiking time: 1–2 hours
Trail surface: Mostly crushed rock, some worn lava, slippery roots
Other trail users: None
Canine compatibility: Leashed dogs permitted
Fees and permits: None for the hike but the fee for parking in the lot is an excellent investment
Schedule: 9 a.m. to 4 p.m., but may vary (for parking)
Land status: Hawai'i Department of Land and Natural Resources
Map: *USGS Honolulu*
Trail Contact: Hawai'i Department of Land and Natural Resources; (808) 973-9782; www.hawaiitrails.org

Finding the trailhead: From the east end of Honolulu drive HI 1 (the Lunalilo Freeway) to exit 23 for Punahou Street and go *mauka* (toward the mountain). Punahou Street soon turns into Manoa Road. Drive Manoa Road for about 3 miles, almost all the way to its end, to a parking lot on the right.

From the west, drive the Lunalilo Freeway to exit 24 for Wilder Avenue. Follow Wilder Avenue past three signals to Punahou Street. Turn right (*mauka*/toward the mountain) on Punahou Street and proceed as above.

You can park for free on the street, but there has been such a high rate of theft from cars at the trailhead in the past that supervised parking is probably worth paying for. **Trailhead GPS:** N21 19.56' / W157 48.02'

The Hike

From the parking lot walk a few hundred yards up the road to a chain-link fence to the right (east) of the entrance to Lyon Arboretum (a great place you might want to visit later). Go through the gate and onto the clearly marked Manoa Falls Trail. You'll be following Waihi Stream all the way to the falls. In the stream gully to your right (east) are several monstrous strangler figs dripping with aerial roots, vines, and creepers, many of which you will recognize as ordinary houseplants like philodendrons and pothos run amok. You'll feel as though you've entered a Tarzan movie.

Cross a tributary creek on a bridge and proceed amid wild ginger, bamboo, huge tree ferns, and tangled thickets of *hau*. This shrub or small tree is a kind of hibiscus found all over the South Pacific. You can see why it is often planted as natural fencing ("*Hau* will I ever get to the other side?"). Its branches are long and spread horizontally, putting down roots whenever they touch the soil, forming a mass of interlocking limbs. The flowers are bright yellow with purple centers, fading to deep orange with darker centers when they fall, as they do after only one day. The bark was used to make rope, and the corky inner wood was used as floats for fishing nets by the early Hawaiians.

The trail gradually becomes steeper and rockier, but in the worst places, metal stair steps have been installed to help you up (and especially down) the hill. Reach an opening in the forest near the base of Manoa Falls just beyond a junction with the 'Aihualama Trail on the left (west). The falls pour over a 60-foot, absolutely vertical cliff into a little pool. People do take dips in the pool, even though a big

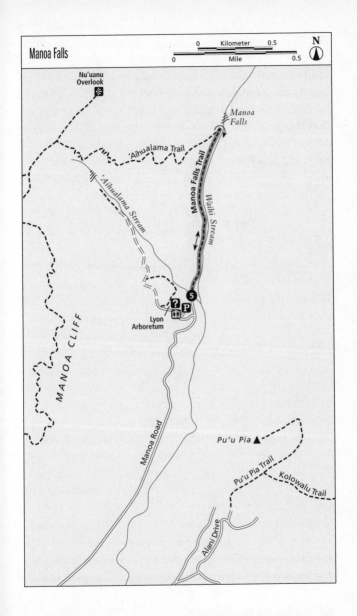

Manoa Falls

Nu'uanu
Overlook

'Aihualama Trail

'Aihualama Stream

Manoa Falls

Manoa Falls Trail

Waihi Stream

5

Lyon
Arboretum

MANOA CLIFF

Manoa Road

Pu'u Pia

Pu'u Pia Trail

Kolowalu Trail

Alani Drive

N

Kilometer

Mile

sign cautions you against going beyond a fence to get closer. A major rock fall in 2002, while harming nobody, created a state of panic about lawsuits among local agencies, so you will be swimming at your own risk.

After you have enjoyed the falls, retrace your steps to the trailhead.

Miles and Directions

0.0   Start

0.8   Junction with the 'Aihualama Trail. A view of the falls is a few steps straight ahead. (N21 20.35' / W157 47.55')

1.6   Return to the trailhead

6 Lyon Arboretum

Right next door to Manoa Falls is an opportunity to see some beautiful ornamental flowers and native Hawaiian vegetation in a more open and manicured setting. There are no slippery tree roots or muddy steps to negotiate in the lower section—a good choice if you didn't bring good walking shoes. You can stroll as far and as long as you like, following any one of several loops, or hike 1.5 miles all the way to the arboretum's upper end to little 'Aihualama Falls, where sturdier footwear is advised.

Distance: 0.4-mile loop
Elevation gain: Negligible
Approximate hiking time: 15 minutes
Trail surface: Cobblestones, grass, gravel, road
Other trail users: None
Canine compatibility: Dogs not permitted
Fees and permits: Donation is requested

Schedule: Open weekdays from 8:00 a.m. to 4:00 p.m.; weekends from 9:00 a.m. to 3:00 p.m.
Maps: Not needed. The visitor center has a map of the garden, or you can go to the arboretum Web site and print a trail map before you go.
Trail contact: Lyon Arboretum; (808) 988-0456; www.hawaii .edu/lyonarboretum

Finding the trailhead: From the east (Waikiki) end of Honolulu follow HI 1 (the Lunalilo Freeway) to exit 23 (Punahou Street) and go *mauka* (toward the mountain). Punahou Street soon turns into Manoa Road. Drive Manoa Road almost all the way to its end, passing the parking lot for Manoa Falls, then continue around three to four switchbacks to the arboretum parking lot on the right (west).

From the west follow the Lunalilo Freeway to exit 24 for Wilder Avenue. Follow Wilder Avenue past three signals to Punahou Street. Turn right on Punahou and proceed as above. Do not park at the arboretum if you plan to hike to Manoa Falls. You will be towed. Restrooms at visitor center. **Trailhead GPS:** N21 19.59' / W157 48.11'

The Hike

Harold L. Lyon was a forester who was responsible for planting the banyan trees that flourish all over Hawai'i. Lyon Arboretum is part of the University of Hawai'i and is devoted to saving and propagating threatened native Hawaiian trees (which banyans are not), along with plants from elsewhere in the tropical world. You might encounter clumps of students engaged in research projects here and there on your walk.

The entrance to the garden is not very well marked. The first building beyond the parking lot is for research. The second is the visitor center, where books and gifts are sold and where you must sign in before beginning your hike.

In the lower section, arranged around a grassy lawn, are a herb and spice garden, a section of plants used by native Hawaiians, and a lily pond among some very showy tropical flowers.

Farther along the main path, on the way to the falls, you can follow various side loop trails leading to Fern Valley, a native forest, collections of bamboos, gingers, palms, and bromeliads (pineapple relatives), and of course, banyans. There are interpretive signs here and there, and many of the plants are labeled if you want to exercise your mind as well as your legs. The screeching that breaks out now and then overhead comes from a flock of wild cockatoos.

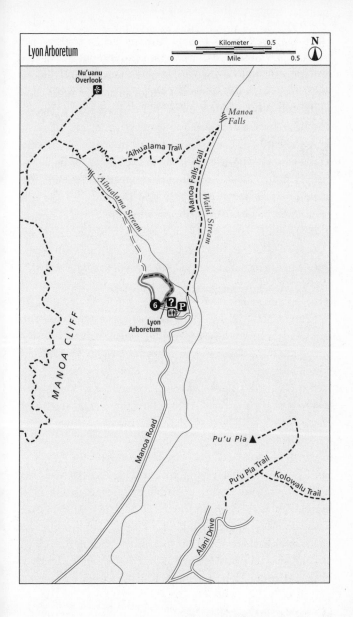

Option: You can follow the main gravel road that runs north-south through the arboretum from the visitor center to within 0.2 mile of the falls. Where the road ends, follow the narrow path around to the left of a patch of sugar cane to the falls. You can pick up the main gravel road from any one of at least a dozen of the garden's loops, or follow it from the left (west) end of the visitor center area all the way to the falls. Round-trip from the visitor center to the falls is 3 miles and will take 1 to 2 hours; expect 250 feet elevation gain. The path may be slippery near the end, and the falls are sometimes dry. Ask at the visitor center.

7 Tantalus-Arboretum Trail

This short, almost flat loop gives you a taste of real tropical forest, even though you are only a few steps away from a suburban road.

Distance: 0.3-mile loop
Elevation gain: 50 feet
Approximate hiking time: 20–30 minutes
Trail surface: Weathered lava
Other trail users: None
Canine compatibility: Leashed dogs permitted
Fees and permits: None

Schedule: Daily during daylight hours
Land status: Hawaii Department of Land and Natural Resources
Map: *USGS Honolulu*
Trail contact: Hawai'i Department of Land and Natural Resources; (808) 973-9782; www.hawaiitrails.org

Finding the trailhead: From the eastern Honolulu area, take HI 1 (the Lunalilo Freeway) to exit 23 for Punahou Street. Head *mauka* (toward the mountains) for 3 blocks to Wilder Avenue. Turn left (west) and drive 3 blocks farther to Makiki Street and turn right (east). At the Y intersection go left on Makiki Heights Drive, then right on Tantalus Drive. The trailhead is just past mile marker 2.5 on the right (east), but hard to spot. There is parking space for three cars just beyond the trailhead. The trailhead is right across the street from a street address marked 3300; there is a trailhead sign. Leave nothing in your car. **Trailhead GPS:** N21 19.33' / W157 49.36'

The Hike

Head slightly uphill from the trailhead sign to find the beginning of the loop, which you can hike in either direction. Starting to the left (clockwise), you first have to nego-

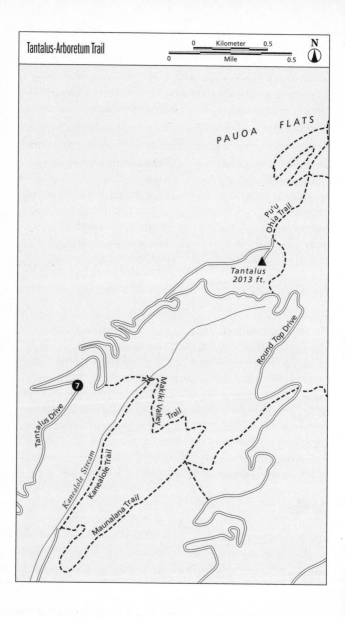

Tantalus-Arboretum Trail

Kilometer
0   0.5
Mile
0   0.5

N

PAUOA FLATS

Pu'u Ohia Trail

Tantalus 2013 ft.

Round Top Drive

7

Tantalus Drive

Kanealole Stream

Kanealole Trail

Makiki Valley Trail

Maunalana Trail

tiate a shallow, usually dry stream gully next to a broken footbridge. After that, the rest is easy walking. The forest is lovely and green, alive with birdsong, dense with ginger, palms, guavas, mosses, and ferns. You'll feel as though you are inside a terrarium.

There are some big banyan trees, one with great buttress roots. These are a common feature of tropical trees, which must grow so quickly and so tall to compete with neighboring trees for sunlight that they need extra support at their bases. They also send aerial roots down to the ground from their branches to make new trunks. Giant escaped houseplants like pothos and philodendron climb every tree, drape themselves over limbs, and dangle long ropy vines back down over the trail, tempting both big and little kids to play Tarzan.

8 Pu'u Ohia (Mount Tantalus)

Pu'u Ohia is the Hawaiian name for Mount Tantalus, the high point on the edge of a volcanic cinder cone. The view from the summit is one of the finest, taking in Diamond Head, Pearl Harbor, the Wai'anae Range, the Ko'olau Range, Nu'uanu Pali, and the Tantalus crater . . . weather permitting, of course.

Distance: 1 mile out and back
Elevation gain: 800 feet
Approximate hiking time: 45 minutes–1.5 hours
Trail surface: Part weathered lava with some stairs, part paved road
Other trail users: None
Canine compatibility: Leashed dogs permitted

Fees and permits: None
Schedule: Daily during daylight hours
Land status: Hawai'i Department of Land and Natural Resources
Map: USGS Honolulu
Trail contact: Hawai'i Department of Land and Natural Resources; (808) 973-9782; www.hawaiitrails.org

Finding the trailhead: From the eastern Honolulu area take HI 1 (the Lunalilo Freeway) to exit 23 for Punahou Street. Head *mauka* (toward the mountain) for 3 blocks to Wilder Avenue. Turn left (west), drive 3 blocks farther to Makiki Heights Drive, and turn right (northeast). At the Y intersection turn left on Makiki Heights Drive, and turn right on Tantalus Drive. Just past mile marker 4.5 look for a big turnout on the right (*makai*/toward the ocean). It is marked by posts painted with red-and-white rings and a couple of trash cans. The trailhead is just across the street. It isn't terribly conspicuous, but there is a sign if you look for it. Do not leave anything in your car.
Trailhead GPS: N21 19.50'/W157 49.17'

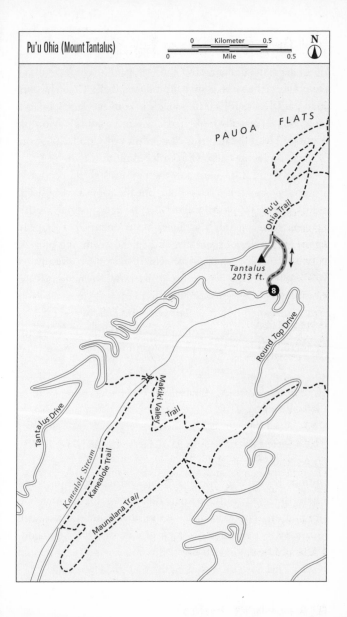

0   Kilometer   0.5

0   Mile   0.5

N

PAUOA   FLATS

Pu'u
Ohia Trail

Tantalus
2013 ft.

8

Round Top Drive

Tantalus Drive

Makiki Valley
Trail

Kaneololo Stream

Kanealole Trail

Maunalana Trail

The Hike

The crater is the remains of O'ahu's last gasp (maybe) of volcanic activity—the same gasp that produced Koko Crater, Koko Head, and Diamond Head—so it's one of the few spots on the island that actually looks like a crater. It's not as obvious as Diamond Head because it is covered in vegetation. Still, you can look down into a bowl from the summit.

It does rain a lot here and the path can be slippery. It's also pretty steep for an easy hike, but the route is very short and the views are worth the effort. The very first part of the climb is a sweaty uphill struggle, but it doesn't last long. It begins on a series of stairs that ends at the beginning of a set of switchbacks, at the end of which the trail continues to wind uphill—but a little more easily now, through a dense bamboo grove. A last short steep pull brings you to a paved road. Turn sharply left (southwest) and follow the road to the top, arriving among lots of telephone towers. Soak up the incredible panorama, then return the way you came.

Miles and Directions

- **0.0** Trailhead
- **0.3** Paved road; turn left (southwest)
- **0.5** Summit and overlook (N 21 19.58'/W 157 48.54')
- **1.0** Return to trailhead

Option: If you want more, turn around on the summit and follow the road north, passing the turnoff to the trail you came up on. The road makes a dip, then climbs past a small concrete structure to an overlook of a sea of waving bamboo. A junction here connects this trail with more of the Honolulu Mauka Trail System, including the trail to Manoa Falls.

9 Pu'u Pia Trail

This hike takes you through a forest of gaudy tropical flowers and singing birds to the top of a local landmark for a great view of the Ko'olau *pali* (cliff), Honolulu, and the sea. It's a steady climb but on a well graded good trail.

Distance: 1.6 miles up and back
Elevation gain: 500 feet
Approximate hiking time: 45 minutes–1 hour
Trail surface: Weathered lava, sometimes muddy
Other trail users: None
Canine compatibility: Leashed dogs permitted
Fees and permits: None

Schedule: Daily during daylight hours
Land status: Hawai'i Department of Land and Natural Resources
Map: *USGS Honolulu*
Trail Contact: Hawai'i Department of Land and Natural Resources; (808) 973-9782; www.hawaiitrails.org

Finding the trailhead: From downtown Honolulu head east on HI 1 (the Lunalilo Freeway) to exit 23 for Punahou Street. Go *mauka* (toward the mountain). Punahou Street turns into Manoa Road. Where Manoa Road splits at a Y intersection, take the right fork onto East Manoa Road and continue to where the road ends at Alani Drive. Turn left (north) on Alani Drive to Woodlawn Drive, and park on the street. Please do not block local residents' driveways. **Trailhead GPS:** N21 19.17' / W157 47.54'

The Hike

Begin at the trail sign on Alani Drive, which almost immediately turns into Alani Lane and becomes very narrow. The pavement ends after you have passed a few houses and

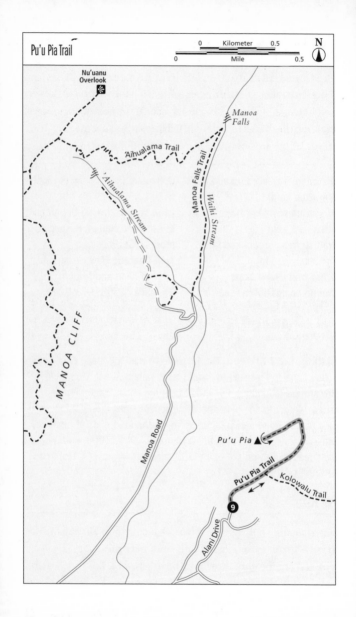

Pu'u Pia Trail

Nu'uanu
Overlook

Manoa
Falls

'Aihualama Trail

Manoa Falls Trail

Waihi Stream

'Aihualama Stream

MANOA CLIFF

Manoa Road

Pu'u Pia ▲

Pu'u Pia Trail

Kolowalu Trail

9

Alani Drive

N

0   Kilometer   0.5

0   Mile   0.5

a graffiti-covered wall. Step over the low cable that blocks vehicle access to the route and find yourself in deep forest all at once, beneath tall dark trees dripping with vines and creepers, most of them escaped houseplants.

The trail splits after only about 0.1 mile, at a sheltered picnic table. The right (east) fork is the Kolowalu Trail. Keep left (northeast) on the Pu'u Pia Trail, which is lined with spectacular gingers and heliconias in varied colors, and white-rumped shamas warble (they really do warble) in the trees.

Ascend easily on footing that seems entirely surfaced with interwoven tree roots. Swing to the left (southwest) and cross a grassy ridge in more open country, where natives like *ohia lehua* and *uluhe* ferns take over, to the top at 2,236 feet. There is a little bench from which to enjoy the view. If the weather is good, you can see out over the Manoa Valley down to sparkling Honolulu and the sea beyond, while the Ko'olau mountains rise behind you in a massive green wall. Return as you came.

Miles and Directions

0.0 Start
0.8 Pu'u Pia (N21 19.31' / W157 47.47')
1.6 Return to Pu'u Pia Trailhead

10 Diamond Head

Diamond Head, or Le'ahi to Hawaiians, is the most famous landmark in all Hawai'i, the classic hike everybody must do when they come to O'ahu. Wilderness it is not. From beginning to end a steady stream of hikers of all ages, sizes, and states of physical fitness (or lack thereof) puffs up and down the steps. For many locals, it's a popular conditioning run. (Yes, run!) The view from the top is superb in all directions, as you would expect.

Distance: 1.6 miles up and back
Elevation gain: 560 feet
Approximate hiking time: 45 minutes–1.5 hours
Trail surface: Partly paved, some dirt, some concrete stairs, and a fairly steep metal spiral staircase
Other trail users: None
Canine compatibility: Dogs not permitted
Fees and permits: Fees are charged for both vehicle and pedestrian entry

Schedule: Open from 6:00 a.m. to 6:00 p.m. daily
Land status: Diamond Head State Monument
Map: The only map you'll need is the excellent one in the brochure you receive as you enter the park.
Trail contact: Hawai'i Department of Land and Natural Resources, Division of State Parks; (808) 587-0300; www.hawaiistateparks.org

Finding the trailhead: This hike may be as easy to reach by TheBus as it is by car if you're already staying in Honolulu or Waikiki. For route information call (808) 848-5555; current schedules are also available at outlets all over town.

If you are driving, you can see Diamond Head from almost any place in Honolulu or Waikiki—unless you are in a canyon of high-rise buildings. The trick is to head toward the mountain, sticking as close

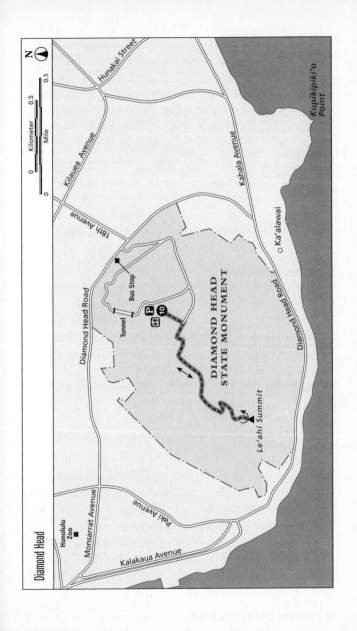

to the coast as you can, and pick up Monsarrat Avenue near the Honolulu Zoo and the east side of Kapiolani Community College. It's a one-way road heading eastward. It turns into Diamond Head Road, which circles the crater. Watch for the well-marked entrance on your right (south). If you reach 18th Avenue, you've gone too far. Drive up the park road, through a tunnel, and emerge at the entrance kiosk and parking lot. Water and restrooms are available near the trailhead. **Trailhead GPS:** N21 15.49' / W157 48.23'

The Hike

This hike is short, and it can be easy if you take it slowly and enjoy cooler weather by starting out early in the morning or as late in the afternoon as possible, allowing yourself enough time to get back down before closing. It can be very hot in the middle of the day. Take water and sunscreen, and good shoes with nonslip soles.

The hike is well described in the brochure you receive at the kiosk as you enter. The maps are detailed and easy to follow, and the accompanying information interesting and entertaining. In a nutshell, you begin along a flat concrete walkway that gradually begins to gain elevation. The concrete ends and a ramp with handrails begins zigzagging more steeply uphill.

Shortly after passing a lookout you climb a stairway of seventy-four steps, go through a dimly though adequately lit tunnel, climb a second staircase, and enter the bottom of the original Fire Control Station. Inside, climb a circular metal staircase to reach the top and squeeze out through a low doorway into the open air. A last set of metal steps takes you to the wonderful 360-degree view overlooking Waikiki, Koko Head, and back toward the misty Ko'olau mountains. Go back down the way you came up.

11 Judd–Jackass Ginger Pool

This may be the most popular short hiking destination on O'ahu, a place for socializing and swimming as much as communing with nature. Nu'uanu Stream flows along the southwest side of the elongated loop and widens into a pretty ginger-lined pool fed by a 10-foot cascade.

Distance: 1-mile loop
Elevation gain: 200 feet
Approximate hiking time: 40 minutes–1 hour
Trail surface: Weathered lava
Other trail users: Mountain bikers
Canine compatibility: Leashed dogs permitted
Fees and permits: None

Schedule: Daily during daylight hours
Land status: Hawai'i Department of Land and Natural Resources
Map: *USGS Honolulu*
Trail contact: Hawai'i Department of Land and Natural Resources; (808) 973-9782; www.hawaiitrails.org

Finding the trailhead: From downtown Honolulu take HI 1 (the Lunalilo Freeway) west for a little more than 1 mile to HI 61 (the Pali Highway) northbound. Turn off the Pali Highway at the Nu'uanu Pali Drive exit, turn right (east) and go for about 1 mile through suburbs to the parking area and trailhead on the right (south). The trailhead is not terribly conspicuous, but it's just past the bridge over the stream, and there are bound to be cars there—possibly so many you'll have to find a spot farther along the road. Theft from parked cars is all too common here. Leave nothing in yours. **Trailhead GPS:** N21 20.49' / W157 49.17'

The Hike

The short loop trail is named for Lawrence Judd, who was a governor of Hawai'i in territorial days, and tradition has it

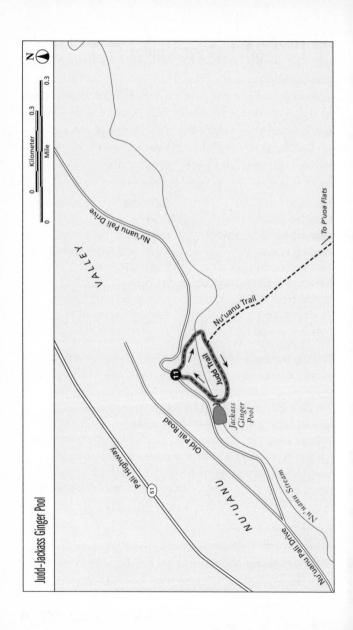

Judd–Jackass Ginger Pool

that somebody grazed a donkey in the grass near the pool at one time. It is often crowded, especially on weekends, and parking is sometimes a problem. The best time for a hike is early in the morning on a weekday. You can walk directly to the pool, or hike the loop the long way round (clockwise), rewarding yourself with a swim toward the end.

Drop down to the stream from the parking lot beneath big banyan trees, and cross Nu'uanu Stream on slippery rocks. Signs on the other side point both ways. For now go right (southwest) and follow the wide trail up through bamboo forest and swamp mahogany (a kind of eucalyptus), then through a grove of Cook pine. Signs at intervals keep you on the trail so you don't end up in somebody's back yard.

Drop down to meet a junction with the Nu'uanu Trail on the left (southeast) at 0.4 mile. It connects with the Honolulu Mauka Trail System, where you can choose from any number of hiking trails if you want to extend your trip. At about 0.7 mile you begin to hear Nu'uanu Stream below. Watch for an iron post on the left (downhill), which guides you to the pool.

The spur down to the pool is steep and slippery. The water is a bit murky, but nobody seems to mind. There is a rope to swing on over the cascade, and plenty of rocks for sitting. Do not dive in though—the pool isn't very deep. Swat a few mosquitoes, sniff the clumps of ginger surrounding the pool, then hike back up the spur to the main trail. This gradually descends to the bank of the stream again, where there are a few more little pools. When you reach the intersection at the stream crossing, you have closed the loop. Cross the stream and hike back uphill to the parking area.

Miles and Directions

0.0 Start

0.4 Junction with Nu'uanu Trail; keep right on the Judd Trail.

0.7 Jackass Pool

1.0 Return to the trailhead

12 Nu'uanu Pali–The Old Pali Highway

The view from the Nu'uanu Pali overlook is truly stunning, but you have to share it with hundreds of chattering tourists and rumbling tour buses unless you walk a bit. With very little effort you can wander past the chaos down the Old Pali Highway and have the views almost to yourself.

Distance: 1.5 miles out and back

Elevation loss: 350 feet

Approximate hiking time: 30 minutes–1 hour

Trail surface: Abandoned paved road

Other trail users: Mountain bikers

Canine compatibility: Leashed dogs permitted

Fees and permits: None

Schedule: Daily during daylight hours

Land status: Nu'uanu Pali State Wayside

Map: *USGS Honolulu*

Trail contact: Hawai'i Department of Land and Natural Resources, Division of State Parks; (808) 587-0166; www .hawaiistateparks.org

Finding the trailhead: From Honolulu drive HI 61 (the Pali Highway) north about 7 miles and exit at the Nu'uanu Pali State Wayside turnoff. If you find yourself inside a tunnel you have gone too far. Drive the access road to where it ends at the parking area for the overlook. Restrooms available at the trailhead. **Trailhead GPS:** N21 21.56' / W157 47.37'

The Hike

This is the site of perhaps the most important battle in Hawaii's history. Nu'uanu Pali is the place where King Kamehameha drove his enemies over the cliff in the battle

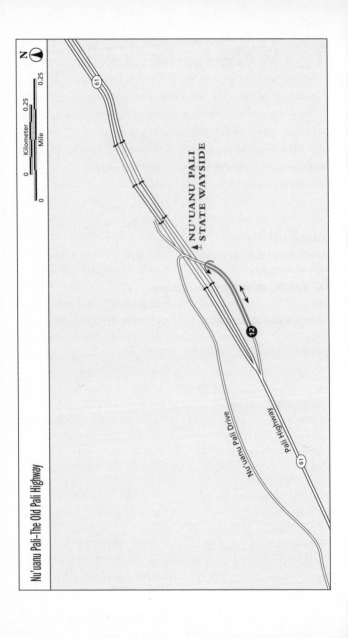

Nu'uanu Pali–The Old Pali Highway

N

0   Kilometer   0.25

0   Mile   0.25

61

NU'UANU PALI
STATE WAYSIDE

12

Nu'uanu Pali Drive

Pali Highway

61

that won him the power to unify the Hawaiian Islands. There are some interesting interpretive panels at the overlook, where you can read about King Kamehameha I, probably the most colorful and celebrated figure in the history of the islands, about the construction of the Pali Highway, and view a map naming the features spread out before you. The Mokapu Peninsula separates Kailua Bay on the right from Kane'ohe Bay on the left, and the ragged cliffs of the Ko'olau mountains flank your viewpoint.

From here, just head downhill to the right of the overlook on the old asphalt road tucked close to the ferny lava cliff, and descend gently among greenery that looks determined to reclaim the mountainside for its own. There are plenty of guavas for summer snacking, along with morning glories, elderberries, and ginger. The road ends where rapacious vegetation and crumbling hillside rubble blocks further (easy) progress. You can see cars emerging from the tunnel below you, and you never really do get away from highway noise, but you feel as though you are more than just physically above it all. When you must, retrace your steps to the parking lot.

13 Maunawili Falls

This is a very popular hike to a pretty little waterfall and pool. You will probably enjoy it more if you get there early in the day. The surrounding area was once farmed by the early Hawaiians, later planted with sugar, coffee, and rubber, and grazed by cattle, but is now lush and green again and blooming with flowers. It is shady most of the way, usually damp and sometimes muddy, with three slippery stream crossings. Do not try this hike if there has been hard steady rain or the water in the stream looks high.

Distance: 2.8 miles out and back
Elevation gain: 420 feet
Approximate hiking time: 2–3 hours
Trail surface: Worn lava, tree roots, rocks, mud
Other trail users: None
Canine compatibility: Leashed dogs permitted
Fees and permits: None
Schedule: Daily during daylight hours

Land status: Hawai'i Department of Land and Natural Resources
Maps: The map published by the Hawai'i DLNR through the *Na Ala Hele* Trail and Access System does show the route, but not in much detail. You can print a map off www.hawaiitrails.org.
Trail contact: Hawai'i Department of Land and Natural Resources; (808) 973-9782; www.hawaiitrails.org

Finding the trailhead: From Honolulu drive HI 1 (the Lunalilo Freeway) to HI 61 (the Pali Highway) northbound. Go through the tunnels, past an intersection with HI 83 (the Kamehameha Highway) and the *first* A'uola Road junction. At the *second* A'uola Road junction, turn right (south) at a signal, then almost immediately turn right (south) on Maunawili Road. The road gradually narrows to one lane and reaches an intersection with Kelewina Street. There is no official trailhead parking, but you can park on Kelewina. Please do not block residents' driveways. The trail begins on a private road at a sign for the trailhead. **Trailhead GPS:** N21 21.33' / W157 45.43'

The Hike

Follow the shady private paved road alongside Olomana Stream, which is audible but not visible, to where the road is very clearly marked CLOSED. Turn right (north) onto the Maunawili Falls Trail, which is fairly flat and wide at first beneath tall straight trees draped with huge houseplants. Alongside the trail you'll see several different kinds of colorful gingers, showy heliconias (lobster claws), and birds-of-paradise, as well as occasional coffee plants left over from agricultural days.

Descend to Maunawili Stream and cross to the right side for the first time . . . carefully. The rocks are slimy. Once across, keep left along the stream bank. Cross the stream twice more within the next 0.5 mile, and continue to climb. There are lots of mango trees dropping fruit all over the place in summer, but you'll have to be quick to beat the locals to them.

After the third stream crossing there is an obscure junction with a narrow trail going uphill to the right (west) and a wider one heading back toward the stream to the left (east). Take the left fork. At streamside you'll find another MAU-NAWILI FALLS TRAIL sign, where you turn right (east) and slop through some mud, then veer away from the stream climbing alternating sets of stairs and tangles of roots. The steps get steeper and steeper until you emerge at last into the sunshine on an open ridge. A trail sign directs you to the left (north), up the ridgeline.

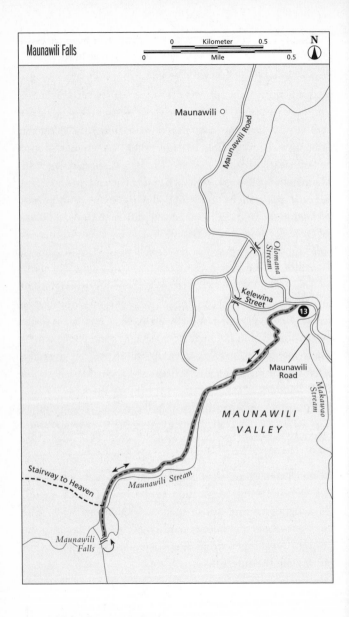

Maunawili Falls

0 ——————— Kilometer ——————— 0.5
0 ——————— Mile ——————— 0.5

N

Maunawili ○

Maunawili Road

Olomana Stream

Kelewina Street

13

Maunawili Road

Makawao Stream

MAUNAWILI VALLEY

Stairway to Heaven

Maunawili Stream

Maunawili Falls

Catch your breath, take in the view down (northwest) to Kane'ohe Bay and up (south/southeast) toward the imposing vertical face of the Ko'olau mountains. At the next junction your trail cuts off to the left (south) and heads steeply downhill. The other, uphill (west) fork begins the Stairway to Heaven, a trail connecting this hike with the Maunawili Trail, a 10-mile route that runs along the face of the *pali* (cliff).

The descent to the stream and the falls is very steep, on big stair steps. At the bottom, in a beautiful forest glade, hop across a smaller stream flowing in from the right (west) to meet the Maunawili Stream and follow the Maunawili Stream's right bank uphill. For the first few yards there is not much trail, just partly submerged rocks, but the route soon begins to look like a trail again. Climb another 50 yards to the pool and the waterfall. It's less than 20 feet high, but in perfect proportion with the pool at its base and the surrounding rock walls. Have a dip in the slightly murky water, then retrace your steps to the trailhead.

Miles and Directions

0.0 Start
1.0 Maunawili Falls turnoff; go left (downhill/south)
1.4 Maunawili Falls (N21 20.59' / W157 46.22')
2.8 Return to trailhead

14 Kuli'ou'ou Valley Trail

A shady stroll takes you through a lush green valley toward the heart of the Ko'olau Range.

Distance: 2 miles out and back
Elevation gain: 350 feet
Approximate hiking time: 45 minutes–1.5 hours
Trail surface: Weathered lava
Other trail users: Mountain bikers and hunters
Canine compatibility: Leashed dogs permitted
Fees and permits: None

Schedule: Daily during daylight hours
Land status: Hawai'i Department of Land and Natural Resources; Kuli'ou'ou State Forest Reserve
Map: USGS Koko Head
Trail contact: Hawai'i DLNR; (808) 973-9782; www.hawaii trails.org

Finding the trailhead: From Honolulu take HI 1 (the Lunalilo Freeway) east. In a very few miles, depending on where you are in Honolulu, the freeway ends and becomes HI 72 (the Kalaniana'ole Highway). Four miles after the freeway ends, turn left (*mauka/ toward the mountain*) on Kuli'ou'ou Road. The street might not be well marked, but there is a signal there. About 1 mile up, in a suburb, turn left (north) where signs on both roads say DEAD END. Follow Kuli'ou'ou Road for a few blocks to Kala'au Place, turn right (east), and go to the end of the street. Park at the curb. **Trailhead GPS:** N21 18.12' / W157 42.27'

The Hike

Pass the stone barrier marked KULI'OU'OU RESERVOIR, sign in on the sheet in the mailbox to your left, and follow the clearly marked trail northward into the valley. In 0.2 mile the trail splits. Your route continues straight ahead (north),

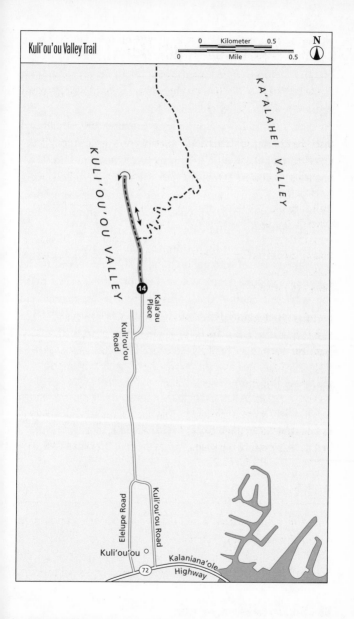

Kuli'ou'ou Valley Trail

Kilometer
0   0.5
0   Mile   0.5

N

KA'ALAHEI VALLEY

KULI'OU'OU VALLEY

14 Kala'au
    Place

Kuli'ou'ou
Road

Elelupe Road

Kuli'ou'ou Road

Kuli'ou'ou

Kalaniana'ole
Highway

72

while the Kuli'ou'ou Ridge Trail cuts off to the right (east). Use a set of built-in boot brushes at this junction to scrape off any noxious weed seeds you might have picked up elsewhere. Hawaii's native vegetation is under siege from aggressive introduced species.

The trail follows alongside a (usually) dry streambed lined with dense ferns and strawberry guava trees. Take your time beside a little stream to savor the ferns and flowers. You're almost certain to hear the clear, melodious song of the shama thrush, and have a good chance of seeing one. They are slender birds with black heads, chestnut fronts, and two bright white feathers along the sides of the tail. You can see a white patch on their rumps when they fly.

After 1 mile of walking on good trail you can cross to the other side of the stream, where a couple of tall cairns mark the way, but beyond this point the trail is not maintained and becomes a muddy, brushy scramble. If you want to see the top of the Ko'olau Range, take much more strenuous Kuli'ou'ou Ridge Trail. Return the way you came.

Miles and Directions

0.0 Start
1.0 End of trail (N21 18.35' / W157 43.33')
2.0 Return to the trailhead

15 Koko Crater Botanical Garden

This is one of the City and County of Honolulu's five botanical gardens, and arguably the most interesting, set as it is inside Koko Crater, the largest cone made of volcanic ash on O'ahu. It is the only one that offers a real "hike," with a beginning and end.

Distance: 2-mile loop
Elevation gain: None
Approximate hiking time: 1–2 hours
Trail surface: Dirt road
Other trail users: None
Canine compatibility: Dogs not permitted
Fees and permits: None

Schedule: Open from sunrise to sunset daily
Map: *USGS Koko Head,* but you really don't need a map
Trail contact: Honolulu Department of Parks and Recreation; (808) 522-7060; www.honolulu .gov/parks/hbg

Finding the trailhead: From Honolulu take HI 1 (the Lunalilo Freeway) east. Once you're out of Honolulu the freeway ends and turns into HI 72 (the Kalaniana'ole Highway). Continue on the Kalaniana'ole Highway for about 8 miles. You'll pass over a saddle between Koko Crater and Koko Head and the Hanauma Bay turnoff on the right (south). Turn left (*mauka*/toward the mountain) onto Kealahou Street. It's not well marked but there is a traffic light. In less than 1 mile a sign says KOKO CRATER BOTANICAL GARDEN. What you'll actually see is a golf course. Turn left (west) anyway and go a few hundred yards to where the road ends at a smaller sign that announces the BOTANICAL GARDEN and KOKO CRATER STABLES. Turn right (north) into the driveway and park near the gate. Outhouse is available. **Trailhead GPS:** N21 18.53' / W157 41.41'

Koko Crater Botanical Garden

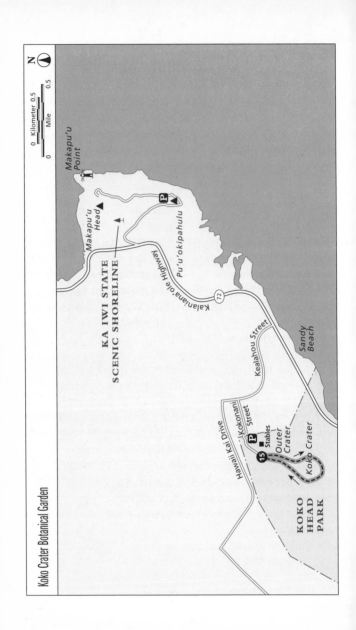

The Hike

Each of Honolulu's botanical gardens has its specialty, and this one features plants of dry lands and deserts all over the world. It's not a trim, well-manicured grassy place, but a more or less wild spot where the plants at least appear to be left alone to be themselves. Yes, you did come to Hawai'i to see things Hawaiian (if you don't already live here), but you are not likely to see such a crazy mix of botanical oddities anyplace else in the world.

Take the loop in either direction; we describe it here clockwise. Walk past the gate and be sure to pick up a free guide to the garden before setting off down the road amid a cloud of fragrance wafting from a forest of plumeria trees of every color imaginable. These are the flowers you're most likely to see in a *lei*. There are also bougainvilleas in masses of color more intense than that of the plumerias.

The American section of plantings includes giant saguaros, fat barrel cacti, and big "old man" cacti with gray beards. The African section has real baobabs from Madagascar, with fat juglike trunks whose leaves and branches seem much too small to fit them. There are sausage trees, dripping with enormous seedpods that look like sausages on steroids. These also have gaudy red-purple flowers in spring.

It's such an exceptional place that as you return to the start of the loop, you'll probably be startled to see housing developments spreading up the hillside like cancerous growths just outside the crater rim.

16 Ka Iwi (Makapu'u Point)

This popular hike offers some of the best sea views on O'ahu, a photogenic lighthouse, and a special bonus from December through April: migrating humpback whales, lots of them, just offshore. It's the easternmost point of O'ahu, affording views southwest back to Koko Crater and Koko Head, and northwest along Waimanalo Bay and out over several islands protected as sanctuaries for seabirds. The dramatic spires of the Ko'olau Range poke up out of the clouds behind.

Distance: 2.5 miles out and back
Elevation gain: 500 feet
Approximate hiking time: 1–2 hours
Trail surface: Paved road
Other trail users: None
Canine compatibility: Leashed dogs permitted
Fees and permits: None
Schedule: Open from 7:00 a.m.
to 7:45 p.m. daily
Land status: Makapu'u Point State Wayside/Ka Iwi State Scenic Shoreline
Map: *USGS Koko Head,* but you don't really need a map
Trail contact: Hawai'i Department of Land and Natural Resources, Division of State Parks; (808) 587-0166; www .hawaiistateparks.org

Finding the trailhead: From Honolulu take HI 1 (the Lunalilo Freeway) east. Once you're out of Honolulu, the freeway ends and becomes HI 72 (the Kalaniana'ole Highway). Continue for about 10 miles, over a saddle between Koko Crater and Koko Head and past the Hawai'i Kai Golf Course. Less than 1 mile past the golf course, after the road makes a sharp curve and begins to climb, watch for a turnoff to the right (east) marked KA IWI. Make the turn, then head down through a valley and back up to the parking area. You'll likely see other cars and people moving up the hillside. There is a second turnoff beyond that just goes to an overlook. If you reach the second turnoff or get to Sea Life Park, you've gone too far. **Trailhead GPS:** N21 18.04' / W157 39.05'

The Hike

This walk is sunny and shadeless, but open to the sea breeze. Take water and sunscreen. Take binoculars too, if you have them.

Start the gentle climb up a hill covered with *koa haole, kiawe* (mesquite), and prickly pear cactus, enjoying ever-improving views back toward the rocky coastline toward Koko Head. If you are here between December and April and notice an excited group staring out to sea, you can bet you'll see humpback whales blowing, breaching, and doing whale things. A little more than 0.5 mile up the trail there is an official whale-watching spot with some public binoculars and an interpretive panel with information about the whales.

At a turn in the road and a break in the cliff on the (left/ north) side, get a glimpse of the mistier windward shore and Waimanalo Beach. After the road curves back to the south side of the point again, watch for the stubby little lighthouse clinging close to the cliff below.

Toward the top you'll find concrete piles and foundations of structures left from World War II, along with a plaque honoring navy pilots who died here in 1942. Ascend between iron railings to a fabulous northward view over an ocean that changes color as it passes over coral reefs, looking out toward Manana (Hawaiian for "rabbit," not Spanish for "tomorrow") Island, and the smaller Kaohikaipu Island. A few steps higher and the whole glorious 360-degree panorama is yours, from Diamond Head to the Ko'olau Range,

Ka Iwi (Makapu'u Point)

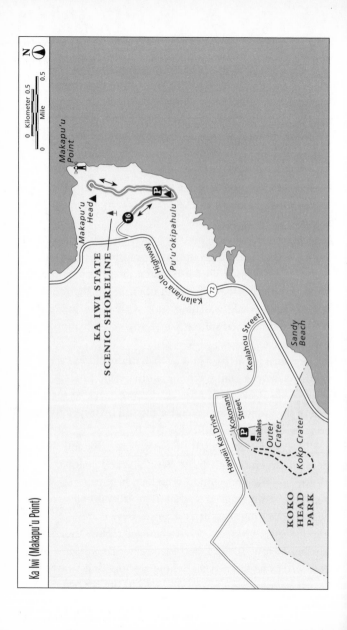

N

0 Kilometer 0.5

0 Mile 0.5

Makapu'u Point

Makapu'u Head

16

Pu'u'okipahulu

KA IWI STATE SCENIC SHORELINE

Kalaniana'ole Highway

72

Kealahou Street

Sandy Beach

Hawaii Kai Drive

Kokonani Street

Stables

Outer Crater

Koko Crater

KOKO HEAD PARK

and, in clear weather, all the way to Moloka'i. You also can look almost straight down upon the little lighthouse, bright white and red against the drab hillside and the blue sea.

From here return to the parking lot.

Miles and Directions

0.0 Start

1.2 Makapu'u Overlook

2.5 Return to trailhead

17 Pu'u o Mahuka Heiau

A *heiau* is a temple or place of worship, usually a raised rectangular platform built from lava rocks by the early Hawaiians. In the old days there would have been altars, huts, and *tikis,* (carved representations of the gods) on top. A *heiau* might be dedicated to a god of war or have some specialized purpose: to propitiate the gods of agriculture or fishing, to teach sacred rituals like the *hula,* to glorify an *ali'i* (chief).

Distance: 0.3-mile loop
Elevation gain: 40 feet
Approximate hiking time: 20–30 minutes
Trail surface: Mostly grass
Other trail users: None
Canine compatibility: Leashed dogs permitted
Fees and permits: None

Schedule: Daily during daylight hours
Land status: Pu'u o Mahuka State Historic Site
Map: *USGS Waimea*
Trail contact: Hawai'i Department of Land and Natural Resources; (808) 973-9782; www.hawaiistateparks.org

Finding the trailhead: From Honolulu drive HI 1 (the Lunalilo Freeway) northwest to HI 2, and head north. Go through the town of Wahiawa to HI 99 (the Kamehameha Highway) and continue north. Just before you reach Haleiwa, the Kamehameha Highway changes from HI 99 to HI 83. Stay on HI 83 to avoid driving through Haleiwa (unless you want to explore the town) and continue north to Waimea Town on Waimea Bay. Watch for the Foodland Market on the right (east), and just before you reach the market turn right, east *(mauka/* toward the mountain) on Pupukea Road. Watch for the HAWAI'I VISITORS BUREAU sign with the *ali'i* in the red cape. Turn right (east) and follow the narrow road to the parking lot. Restroom near the parking lot.
Trailhead GPS: N21 38.28' / W158 03.31'

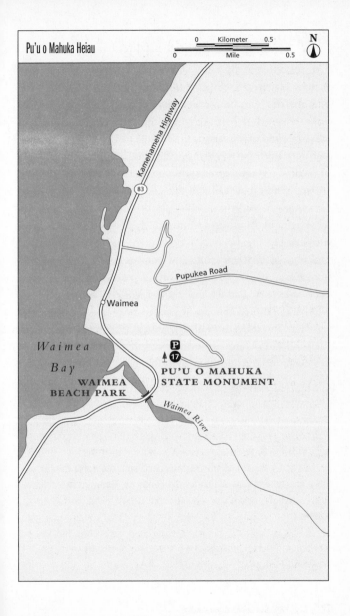

Pu'u o Mahuka Heiau

0   Kilometer   0.5
0   Mile   0.5

N

Kamehameha Highway

83

Pupukea Road

Waimea

Waimea

Bay

WAIMEA
BEACH PARK

P
17

PU'U O MAHUKA
STATE MONUMENT

Waimea River

The Hike

The foundations of many *heiaus* can be found all over the islands, places of both scientific and spiritual interest. This one sits on a lonely knoll above Waimea, which was an important material and religious center in the old days. It is said to be the oldest heiau on O'ahu and was a site of human sacrifice. It's a lonely, windswept, but beautiful spot with a view of the sea, Ka'ena Point, and the Wai'anae mountains, a place where you can still feel the presence of the ancient Hawaiians if you try.

The trail is mostly a smooth path worn in the grass surrounding the heiau. At the upper end is an altar with offerings of flowers, fruit, and coins left by contemporary Hawaiians. Please do not disturb anything, and be sure to heed the KAPU (forbidden) signs. This is a sacred place as well as a National Historical Landmark.

Take the time to read the several interpretive panels at the trailhead. There are drawings and explanations of how the heiau looked and the rituals that took place there in the 1770s, as well as some fascinating information about early Hawaiian life.

18 Ka'ena Point North

This walk follows a beautiful shoreline, with tide pools to explore and endangered species of Hawaiian flowers to examine along the way. From December to May you are almost guaranteed sightings of nesting albatross and migrating humpback whales. You can sometimes spot rare Hawaiian monk seals on the rocks. There is no shade or water and it can be hot even with the sea breeze. Take lots of water and sunscreen.

Distance: 5 miles out and back
Elevation change: None
Approximate hiking time: 2–3 hours
Trail surface: Dirt road
Other trail users: Mountain bikers and all-terrain vehicles as far as the boundary of the Ka'ena Point Natural Area Reserve
Canine compatibility: Dogs not permitted
Fees and permits: None

Schedule: Daily during daylight hours
Land status: Ka'ena Point State Reserve
Map: USGS Ka'ena
Trail contact: Hawai'i Department of Land and Natural Resources; (808) 973-9782; www.hawaiistateparks.org, http://hawaii.gov/dlnr/dofaw/nars/reserves/oahu

Finding the trailhead: From Honolulu drive HI 1(the Lunalilo Freeway) west to HI 2, and continue toward Wahiawa. Turn west on HI 99 toward Schofield Barracks, then keep left (northwest) on HI 930 (the Farrington Highway). Follow the Farrington Highway to its end. Highway numbers are not prominently displayed, but you will pass Dillingham Airfield on the final leg to the trailhead. **Trailhead GPS:** N21 34.44' / W158 14.14'

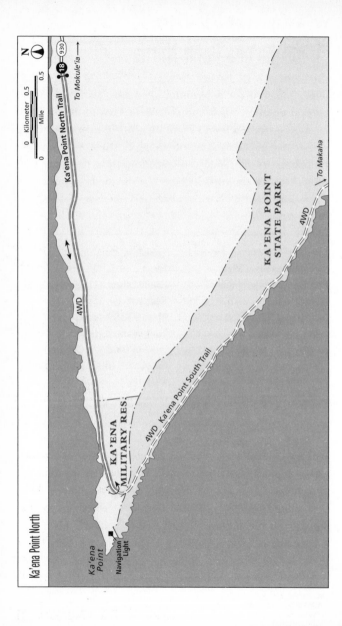

Ka'ena Point North

N

0 Kilometer 0.5
0 Mile 0.5

Ka'ena Point North Trail

18 930

To Mokule'ia →

4WD

KA'ENA
MILITARY RES.

Ka'ena
Point

Navigation
Light

4WD Ka'ena Point South Trail

KA'ENA POINT
STATE PARK

4WD

To Makaha

The Hike

You can get to Ka'ena Point by following the terrible "main" dirt road that continues past the trailhead gate, or you can follow one of the many four-wheel-drive tracks that wind along the beach. You can also just follow the shoreline. Of course, it's cooler and more scenic the closer you are to the sea, but it is much longer. The distance of 5 miles is measured along the main road.

The cliffs to your left (south) are a thousand shades of green and the sea a thousand shades of blue, with patches of red Hawaiian dirt and white surf in between. There are lots of rock shelves and tide pools, but watch out for sneaky waves while exploring them. Among the tire tracks lots of tough little succulent native beach plants have managed to hang on, and at about 2 miles there is an isolated grove of sisal (agave) plants, giant lettuces with long skinny flowering stalks sticking up. These are not native but escapees from cultivation.

The road is finally blocked even to all-terrain vehicles, and especially to dogs, as you reach the entrance to the natural area reserve. Please heed the signs and stay on trails. There is so little of this pristine environment left, you won't want to step on anything fragile. Enter a zone of white sand dunes held in place by carpets of beach *naupaka,* little blue morning glories, apricot-colored *ilima,* and the beautiful and endangered *'ohai,* a low shrub with outsize red pealike flowers. There is a clearly defined trail that makes a little loop around the dunes.

If you are fortunate enough to be here in late winter or early spring, you'll find Laysan albatross, huge, gull-like birds that spend most of their lives over open ocean, nesting all around you among the *naupaka*. They come to land only to breed.

At the very point itself, beyond the navigation light, you can sometimes spot endangered Hawaiian monk seals basking on the rocks, and if you're very lucky indeed, catch sight of the blow or breach of migrating humpback whales. Even without the exciting fauna, it's a thrill to watch the waves coming toward you from two directions, crashing together below the point.

When you have had enough—is that possible?—retrace your steps to your car.

Miles and Directions

- **0.0** Start where the end of the road is blocked by a gate
- **2.5** Ka'ena Point (N21 34.30' / W158 16.52')
- **5.0** Return to the trailhead

19 Ka'ena Point South

Don't miss this one. It is an easy walk on a stunning shore-line, with possible sightings of nesting albatross, rare monk seals, and even whales. There are endangered species of native Hawaiian flowers, tide pools, and blowholes. The point itself, in native Hawaiian belief, is where the souls of the dead leave Earth for the afterworld.

Distance: 5 miles out and back
Elevation change: None
Approximate hiking time: 2–3 hours
Trail surface: Mostly dirt road
Other trail users: Mountain bikers and all-terrain vehicles only at the beginning and end
Canine compatibility: Dogs not permitted
Fees and permits: None
Schedule: Daily during daylight hours
Land status: Ka'ena Point Natural Area Reserve

Map: *USGS Ka'ena*
Trail contact: Hawai'i Department of Land and Natural Resources; (808) 973-9782; www.hawaiistateparks.org, http://hawaii.gov/dlnr/dofaw/nars/reserves/oahu
Special considerations: According to local police, vehicles at the trailhead suffer *daily* break-ins, even though it is patrolled as frequently as the authorities can manage. Better to park an extra 0.5 mile farther back near the lifeguard station. Leave nothing in your car.

Finding the trailhead: From Honolulu take HI 1 northwest all the way past Kapolei, where HI 1 becomes HI 93 (the Farrington High-way). Follow the Farrington Highway to its end at the trailhead. There is no sign or official trailhead, just the end of the pavement. **Trailhead GPS:** N21 33.22' / W158 14.55'

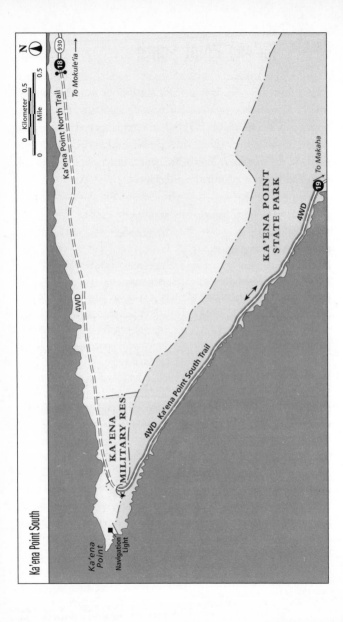

Ka'ena Point South

The Hike

The hike begins at the foot of the cliff, upon which squats a white object that looks like Paul Bunyan's golf ball (actually one of the domes of the nearby military satellite tracking station). The hillside *mauka* (toward the mountain) is mostly covered with *koa haole* and other dry scrubby plants. *Makai* (toward the sea) is one of the most wild and wonderful shorelines ever. Clear turquoise water breaks into waves that thrash the rugged black lava cliffs. There are blowholes and sea arches and endless tide pools filled with sea creatures. If you choose to explore some of these, stay alert for big waves that can sneak up on you.

As you hike a red and white pole topped with a light appears on the point, and you'll notice underfoot a series of railroad ties, all that's left of a railroad that used to run all the way around the point. Reach the rockslide that closed the road that replaced the old railroad. A sign warns that the trail is closed ahead due to hazardous conditions, though nobody pays any attention to it. A trail has been worn through the fallen rock, and at one point, a couple of sturdy boards span a broken section of the cliff, with good lava handholds. There's a lava tube here too, where molten lava flowed under the ground and out into the sea.

As you near the point you'll enter Ka'ena Point Natural Area Reserve. Please heed the signs and stay on trails to preserve the pristine environment. White sand dunes are held in place by carpets of beach *naupaka*, little native blue morning glories, apricot-colored *ilima*, and the beautiful and endangered *'ohai,* a low shrub with outsize red pealike flowers. A clearly defined trail that makes a little loop around the dunes at the point.

In late winter or early spring you'll also see nesting Laysan albatross, huge, gull-like birds that spend most of their lives over the open ocean, coming to land only to breed.

At the point itself, beyond the lighthouse, you can sometimes spot endangered Hawaiian monk seals and, if you're very lucky indeed, catch a sight of migrating humpback whales. You'll also enjoy watching the waves crashing below the point.

When you have had enough or, more likely, run out of time, retrace your steps to your car.

Miles and Directions

0.0   Start where the pavement ends
2.5   Ka'ena Point (N21 34.30' / W158 16.52')
5.0   Return to the trailhead

20 Wahiawa Botanical Garden

This is one of the five gardens of the Honolulu Botanical Gardens, operated by Honolulu's Department of Parks and Recreation. Each one is part of a different environmental setting, and all are worth visiting. Wahiawa is particularly congenial to tropical moisture-loving plant species.

Distance: About 0.5 mile on a double loop (or as long as you like)
Elevation gain: 40 feet
Approximate hiking time: 20 minutes to as long as you like
Trail surface: Some paved path, some packed dirt
Other trail users: None
Canine compatibility: No dogs permitted

Fees and permits: None
Schedule: Open daily from 9:00 a.m. to 4:00 p.m. (closed Dec 25 and Jan 1)
Map: *USGS Hau'ula,* but you don't really need a map
Trail contact: Honolulu Department of Parks and Recreation; (808) 621-5463 or (808) 522-7060; www.honolulu.gov/parks/hbg

Finding the trailhead: From anywhere in Honolulu drive HI 1 (the Lunalilo Freeway) north to HI 2. Continue north to HI 80 (the Kamehameha Highway). At the town of Wahiawa, turn right (east) onto California Avenue. The garden is on the left at 1396 California Avenue. Restrooms at the entrance. **Trailhead GPS:** N21 30.00' / W158 01.18'

The Hike

This twenty-seven-acre park surrounds a section of Kaukonahua Stream, the longest stream in Hawai'i. Its mid-range elevation and its temperature range of 52 to 80 degrees are congenial to moisture-loving species. This park has several

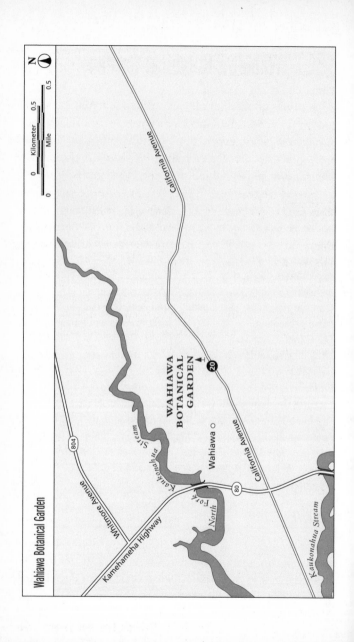

Wahiawa Botanical Garden

sections devoted to different geographic parts of the tropics, and different groupings of plants like heliconias, palms, and bamboos.

It's tranquil to stroll the paths that wind here and there around displays, then drop down into the wilder, less-manicured ravine beside the more formal park. You can make a kind of double loop: one above in the manicured section, another below in the ravine.

Some of the special inhabitants include the cinnamon tree, whose refreshing spicy smell will make its presence known before you read the label. The autograph tree has thick, flat leaves, and if a message—or more often, lovers' initials—are scratched on their surfaces, the scratches scar over and become more or less permanent since the tree retains its leaves for a long time. Its bumpy main limbs may grow upward, outward from the trunk, or dive down to the ground and come back up again in an irregular fashion, making it awkwardly sculptural.

When you have seen enough, return to the garden entrance.

About the Author

Suzanne Swedo, director of W.I.L.D., an adventure travel company, has backpacked the mountains of every continent. She has led groups into the wilderness for more than twenty-five years and teaches wilderness survival and natural sciences for individuals, schools, universities, museums, and organizations such as Yosemite Association and the Sierra Club. She is author of *Best Easy Day Hikes Yosemite National Park, Hiking Yosemite, Hiking California's Golden Trout Wilderness,* and *Adventure Travel Tips,* all FalconGuides. She lectures and consults about backpacking, botany, and survival on radio and television, as well as in print.

WHAT'S SO SPECIAL ABOUT UNSPOILED, NATURAL PLACES?

Beauty   Solitude   Wildness   Freedom   Quiet   Adventure
Serenity   Inspiration   Wonder   Excitement
Relaxation   Challenge

There's a lot to love about our treasured public lands, and the reasons are different for each of us. Whatever your reasons are, the national **Leave No Trace** education program will help you discover special outdoor places, enjoy them, and preserve them—today and for those who follow. By practicing and passing along these simple principles, you can help protect the special places you love from being loved to death.

THE PRINCIPLES OF **LEAVE NO TRACE**

- Plan ahead and prepare
- Travel and camp on durable surfaces
- Dispose of waste properly
- Leave what you find
- Minimize campfire impacts
- Respect wildlife
- Be considerate of other visitors

Leave No Trace is a national nonprofit organization dedicated to teaching responsible outdoor recreation skills and ethics to everyone who enjoys spending time outdoors.

To learn more or to become a member, please visit us at www.LNT.org or call (800) 332-4100.

Leave No Trace, P.O. Box 997, Boulder, CO 80306

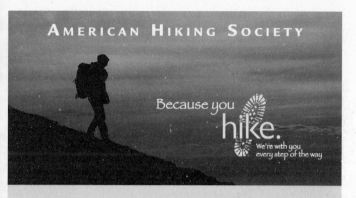